The River Loxley

from emergence to confluence

words Ron Clayton

photographs Mark Rodgers

Text and Photograph copyright 2009 © Ron Clayton & Mark Rodgers and reference

ISBN 9781905278329

Printed in 2009 by Pickards.org.uk

Published by youbooks.co.uk

11 Riverside Park, Sheaf Gardens, Sheffield S2 4BB

Telephone 0114 275 7222

www.youbooks.co.uk

Printed by

Pickards.org.uk

Local studies library reference for photos

w00394 (Dale Dyke), s06033 (Annie Thorpe), w00409 (Chapmans house), w00419 (Wisewood Forge), t02347 (Malin Bridge), s07549 (Hillsborough Bridge).

OS Maps have kindly given permission for use of 5 of their maps

Strines Reservoir

Dale Dyke Reservoir

Agden Reservoir

The River Loxley emerges in the north west of Sheffield on the moorland above Low Bradfield. It flows easterly through Damflask Reservoir and is joined by the River Rivelin at Malin Bridge, before flowing into the River Don at Owlerton, in Hillsborough. The river provided the initial course of the Great Sheffield Flood, which happened after the Dale Dyke Reservoir embankment collapsed just before midnight on 11th March 1864.

Bradfield

Dam Flask

Loxley Valley

Horses near Gibraltar Rocks

The River Loxley

Why 'Loxley' ? It is first recorded, according to Peter Harvey, as Lockeslay or Lokkeslay, in the 1400's. Its conjectural meaning is the clearing or glade in the woods or forest, belonging to Locc, a similar origin to Wadsley. Interestingly enough Sir Walter Scott uses 'Locksley' in naming the outlaw in Ivanhoe.

The four reservoirs which surround Bradfield are fed by numerous tributaries, rivulets and springs from the surrounding moors. With the rather alien backdrop of conifers the area resembles the border areas of England and Scotland, straddled by Hadrian's Wall, and indeed that's what it was, just that, a frontier zone.

How appropriate then to see the Strines Reservoir overlooked, not only by horses but its own Pele or Peel Tower as a refuge against raiders.

This of course is the famous local 'Folly' built by Charles Boot in 1927 to provide work for the unemployed. Its only military use, I believe, was by the Bradfield Home Guard in WWII. One can imagine Private Frazer recounting, one of his eye rolling, spooky tales at dead of night in this isolated spot!

Strines Reservoir

One of four new reservoirs built in the second half of the nineteenth century to provide for Sheffield's increasing water needs, Strines was completed in 1869 covering an area of 22 hectares. The dam wall is 95.5 feet high with a length of 1082.7 feet. It has a capacity of 452,900,000 gallons of water.

Strines Reservoir

Leofzky the Llama

Alice the Donkey near Gibraltar Rocks

This alert looking llama is, of course, not native to these parts. Leofzky the llama was brought to this country from Peru when he was only one year old. He immediately struck up a relationship with Alice, a donkey who at 23 years old had just lost her mother who had reached the ripe old age of 40. They became inseparable and now live happily in a field near Gibraltar Rocks.

I'm not too sure whether you eat llamas. They have other uses, their wool. However, as this vigilant specimen shows, llamas make excellent sheep dogs and are very protective of their flocks, with a tendency to spit at foxes who get too close.

The most famous llama is of course the Dalai Lama, who hails from Tibet and not South America and is a very respected and loved fellow with glasses. He too is not native to the area.

As these pictures of Dale Dyke show, much of the surrounds of the subsequently rebuilt dam are picturesque for the most part with their conifers and Victorian shrubbery and solid masonry and ironwork. It's a scene far removed from the sparsely treed, rather harsh landscape that is the backdrop to the scenes of the aftermath of the Flood recorded by long dead photographers. Its only on the upland slopes above the dam that you find echoes of what must have been a rather wild and inhospitable environment in which the navvies who built Dale Dyke found themselves having to work.

The CLOB stones, four in number, and so named because they mark the 'Centre Line, Old Bank', embankment of Dale Dyke are the only echoes on the site of the massive wall that ruptured just before midnight of the 11th March 1864.

Victorian footbridge at Dale Dyke

The memorial to the victims of the Great Sheffield Flood of 1864 was set up by the Bradfield Historical Society whose secretary, Malcolm Nunn, is the Bradfield Parish Council Archivist, an authority on the Flood, all things Bradfield and a good egg. Opened by Martin Olive, another Flood expert and former Local Studies Guru at the

Centre Line, Old Bank stone

Sheffield Central Library (Martin is also one of those Sheffielders, like Malcolm, who never looks any older). The memorial is the first modern acknowledgement of what has been termed 'The Forgotten Flood' and perhaps the most aptly placed.

Dale Dyke Reservoir

Dale Dyke Reservoir was constructed by the Sheffield Waterworks Company 1859-1864. It was built to supply drinking water and also to power the mills further downstream. After the dam wall was breached in 1864 causing the Great Sheffield Flood it was rebuilt in 1875 to hold 486,000,000 gallons of water which was a reduction in the previous capacity of 712,000,000 gallons. The new wall was built further back to a height of 80 feet with a length of 900 feet.

No one could write a book about the River Loxley or the Loxley Valley without, at least, mentioning, The Great Sheffield Flood or Inundation of March 1864.

This is of course, a book about a river and its hinterland, not about the flood. Where I have touched upon this greatest of Sheffield peacetime disasters, I have deliberately avoided referring back or consulting sources and authorities such as the doyen of them all, Samuel Harrison (let's face it I'd need a ouija board, he's been dead long enough), Geoffrey Amey's 'The Collapse of the Dale Dyke Dam', our own Malcolm Nunn and others of that ilk, Peter Machan and Martin Olive (all of whom I have had the pleasure of knowing for many years).

I can never resist Michael Armitage's excellent Sheffield Flood webpage with its haunting 'New York Mining Disaster 1941' theme, which has the same effect on me as Ivor Emmanuel leading the 'gallant 24th' of Rorke's Drift in their rendition of 'Men Of Harlech'. I'm ashamed to say I haven't yet seen the 'Forgotten Flood' by Phil Parkin, introduced by another illustrious Welshman, Rony Robinson.

If any of my comments re the events of 11th/12th March 1864 require a more valid interpretation then I'll stand corrected. After all what can you expect from someone, who as a kid, wondered whether the green on the stone walls adjacent to Dam Flask was the result of 'The Great Flood'?

Plaque in remembrance of those who perished

March 1864 photograph showing devastation caused by the breach

Bradfield Moors towards
Agden Reservoir

Agden Reservoir

Completed in 1869 the Agden Reservoir was built to collect water from the moorland around Bradfield. It holds 559,000,000 gallons of water and covers an area of 25 hectares. The dam wall is 98.4 feet high and 1148.3 feet wide. The dam is fed by Hobson Moss Dyke and Emlin Dyke which flow off Broomhead and Bradfield Moors. It is ringed by a 3.5 mile walk around Low Bradfield taking in Agden Bog.

Height Marker

These pictures show the dam height marker close to the Agden Reservoir embankment.

View of Agden Reservoir embankment

Bradfield - Village and Parish.

Well what can you say? Is this the England that John Major once conjured up . . . of old maids and warm beer and the crack of leather on willow?

Well there's an ice cream van and cricket pitch where Yorkshiremen play that great leveller of a game, like only Yorkshiremen can . . . hard and to win, in the spirit of Trueman, Close, Ilingworth and Boycott. There is a duck pond too, but you shouldn't feed the ducks because it ruins their figures.

The largest parish in England, stretching from Stannington to Ladybower, almost fifteen thousand souls as the C of E would put it. If you want to appreciate or understand Bradfield, from a visitor's or outsider's point of view, then walk through the churchyard of St. Nicholas and note the Siddons and Brammalls and other local names and gaze upon the gravestones of Bradfield folk who trod this ground in the 1600s. Note the poppies on the memorials to two generations of Bradfielders who fought for King and Country, some of whom didn't come back. Watch the sheep and cows graze peacefully.

Note the younger generation feeding their border terriers bacon and sausage outside the Valley Cafe on a Sunday before they go shooting, or at the age of ten, having total knowledge of their father's land and unlike Mark and I, being totally unruffled by inquisitive cows, while their brother rides a quad bike round that same Old Wheel Farm.

Hear their voices in the choir and smell the flowers in the church, see them relaxing or working in the village pubs or catching the quirky but so civilised buses or at a barn dance on the premises where you can buy Our Cow Molly's ice cream. Bradfield is an ancient and beautiful place but it is very much South Yorkshire, so much so that you forget you are actually in the Peak National Park. Bradfield isn't in our consciousness as part of the 'golden frame' of Sheffield ie those Derbyshire villages which make a living from tourists, walkers and climbers, caverns, castles and blue john.

But it's changing. Gone are those awful privies that you used to have to endure when fishing Dam Flask. The Nurseries down the valley do Sunday roasts while Bradfield Post Office is positively Bohemian with its soups, lattes, cake and longer opening hours. There are more walkers and runners, not mere spectators, around the cricket ground.

Would it take to tourism like its Derbyshire cousins? Well that's up to the folk of Bradfield, who remind me in some respects of what Dr H Kirk-Smith, former vicar of Wamsley, wrote about the old villagers of his beloved manor, 'a hardy, freedom loving people, independent and self reliant'.

Characters like Mary who used to graft hard on her milk round and behind the pumps of the Shoulder and Rivelin, Maurice, who I see on the Hillsborough bound bus at the same time every morning and ex Councillor Bancroft, who used to sleep, dream and breathe Bradfield and its people.

Bradfield likes to keep the yawning maw of the biggest village at arm's length and proclaims its identity and pride by its carved roadside markers and its flowers.

Above all Bradfield is the England that Shakespeare and Kipling wrote about, it's the Queen's England, as it was the King's England. As it will be again.

Continuity in a changing world – may it ever be so - in autumn, winter, spring and summer.

Bradfield

Agden Beck flowing beneath the Smithy Road Bridge from the Agden Reservoir meets the Dale Dyke Beck flowing from Dale Dyke under Mill Lee Road Bridge. These two becks form the Mill Pond at Bradfield which then flows onwards to Dam Flask as the River Loxley

Victorian Postbox at Bradfield

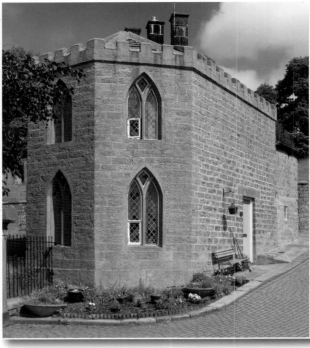

Still in use today and something Sir Rowland Hill would be proud of, unlike the crazy idea to rename the former Royal Mail 'Consignia', closing Post Offices and scrapping that most quintessential piece of British street furniture, the telephone box in its splendid Post Office Red. One of the themes of this celebration and exploration of the Loxley is continuity and this is mirrored in the discovery by Mark Rodgers of a postbox for every British Monarch since Victoria Regina down the valley – (except Edward VIII who does have a box in Sheffield 6 - one of only three in Sheffield). That e-mail and texting will never catch on you know.

Erected to provide shelter for the watchers over the recently interred dead. You can imagine the long, lonely vigils by candlelight of church officials or relatives of the deceased to prevent disinterment of fresh corpses, by medical students or the professional 'resurrection men', at dead of night while the wind whistled over the brooding earthworks of Bailey Hill and gravestones of St Nicholas Churchyard.

Until the passing of the Anatomy Act in 1832 there was no way that the demand for corpses for dissection and research by the increasing number of medical schools could be met by legal means.

The chief suspect for body snatching in nineteenth century Sheffield was the noted local surgeon, Dr Hall Overend, who opened the town's first medical school in1829 and who had

family living in Wamsley. His portrait hangs in the Cutler's Hall and the Public House on Orchard Street called 'The Museum' refers to Overend's collection of anatomical specimens. Hostility towards bodysnatching or suspicion of such activity saw the firing of the Sheffield Medical School in 1835 and also the Wardsend Cemetery disturbances of 1862.

Looking up from Low Bradfield to what was once known as Kirk Town and is now High Bradfield, with the largely 15th Century St. Nicholas Church, with its stained glass, oak, stone and brass. A beautiful church, lovingly and intimately described by Julia Hatfield of Mousehole Forge, noted local historian, in her recent guide. Spectacular when floodlit at night and a cultural as well as spiritual focus for the local community.

Curious sheep graze amongst the gravestones of the extensive churchyard – the perfect and ecologically sound method of keeping the grass short.

Gazing out across Bradfield, this gargoyle is meant to scare off evil spirits or even Old Nick himself. Its stonework is a nice contrast with the late nineteenth century metal work dated 1893. Supernatural influences are cited in local folklore regarding the position of St. Nicholas Church and the gargoyle reflects this tradition.

St. Nicholas Church gargoyle

Bradfield and its vicinity have several mysterious earthworks and monuments. These include Bailey Hill, behind St. Nicholas. Previously regarded as a Roman Burial Treasure Mound, Dark Age assembly point, or a religious site. It is now generally accepted as a Norman Motte and Bailey Castle.

The tradition that the castle on Castle Hill was a defensive earthwork goes back to Hunter and Addy, hence its name. These days it is regarded as a natural but still impressive feature as one reaches High Bradfield.

This Saxon Cross was unearthed in a field in Low Bradfield in the late nineteenth century and later placed in St. Nicholas Church, Bradfield in 1886. Presumably the field was somewhere near the former Cross Inn (now Cross Cottage). The Cross Inn was a lovely little pub with a piano but closed sometime ... well nobody seems quite sure.

I recently had the pleasure of reading a lovely and well researched history of St. Nicholas Church by John and Julia Hatfield. It's such a good read that I never noticed that the pages had been stapled in the wrong order!

The cross is thought to be ninth century and was probably pulled down during the Puritan religious controversies under Elizabeth the First or during the English Civil War (or 'Great Rebellion' as Clarendon referred to it). If stones could speak, what a tale this one could tell.

Saxon Cross

Castle Hill, Bradfield

At one time driving up the Loxley Valley and Bradfield Dale, as far as the former Haychatter, practically all you could sup was Whitbread Trophy and Tankard. That's now changed with Bradfield Brewery at Watt House Farm. Appreciative palates relish Bradfield Blonde in particular and the smart millstone monogrammed glasses reflect a class act. As a result and with the handy and economical bus service provided by South Yorkshire Community Transport the area is becoming a venue for the more discerning and pleasant beer drinker.

Larry the Lamb

Nags Head, Stacey Bank

The flagship of Bradfield Brewery and the best
place to pick up a local Blonde (a brew of real ale).
Almost in the yard of the adjacent farm and a
comfortable little pub of the old school.

Winter in the Upper Loxley Valley

Dam Flask Reservoir

'If a picture paints a thousand words' then these images of Dam Flask make these few words of mine superfluous.

Whether the reservoir and its surrounding landscape is etched into clarity by snow that makes us long for the coats of its patient sheep and reach for the comfort of drinking chocolate, fleece, gloves and daft hat; or the lush greenness of an English Summer with scudding yachts, peaceful cows, blue skies and hanging cotton wool clouds and gentle warmth on my ageing bones; or more interestingly, exhibits the coppers, rusts and vivid life affirming scarlets of that most dependable of all seasons, Autumn – the Flask is the most recreational and accessible water of all the Loxley's neighbours.

On bus, car, foot or horse, your eyes are drawn to it, a focus for activity or just lazy contentment with which to watch the world go by.

Dam Flask at dusk

Dam Flask was completed in 1896. Constructed of local stone, it was originally a compensation reservoir to ensure continuous flow to the River Loxley downstream. The hamlet called Dam Flask was washed away in the Great Flood. Popular with walkers, the dam is also used by anglers and three rowing clubs: Sheffield Rowing Club, The University of Sheffield Rowing Club and Sheffield Hallam University Rowing Club. The dam holds 4,250,900 gallons of water, covers an area of 47 hectares and has a wall 91.9 feet high and 1312.3 feet long.

Two views of Dam Flask

above: The Rowing Clubs – below: Spring on the Nature Trail

above: Sailing on Dam Flask – below: Calm waters

Dam Flask in early spring

Sunshine after the rain at Dam Flask ▶

View of Dam Flask from Ughill Heights

Cattle relaxing on Ughill Heights

Warm sheep at Dam Flask ▶

Dam Flask at sunset

Dam Flask in Autumn

A stormy day at Dam Flask with a low water level

A calm day at Dam Flask ▶

Autumn turns to Winter at Dam Flask

Early morning
stillness at
Dam Flask

Derelict Farm at Dam Flask

Like so many areas of the valley, there's a hint of mystery in this abandoned farm on its lower slopes. Is there any remnant of the lost hamlet of Dam Flask with its bridge and inn where Stephenson Fountain stopped to have his saddle girth repaired? Is this South Yorkshire's lost Lyonesse?

No.... leave that to Ladybower.

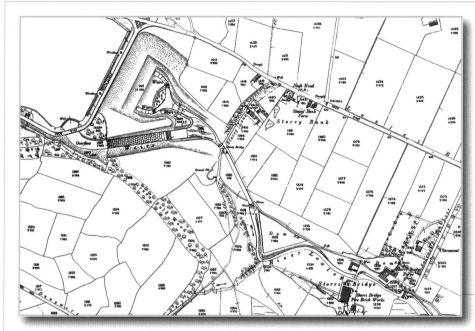

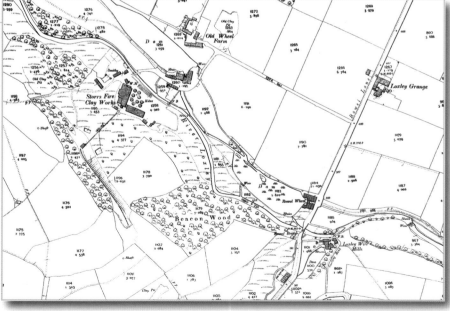

OS maps from 1905 show the course of the River Loxley from Dam Flask to Rowell Lane

Loxley Valley

River Loxley continues at Dam Flask embankment ▶

Because of the aftermath of the Great Flood of 1864 and the subsequent compensation payments that reinvigorated the numerous and varied water powered industrial activities that the Loxley Valley was home to, the valley now retains in situ more extensive traces of its industrial archaeology than any of the other Sheffield rivers. These vary in size from wheels such as the massive, sadly rusting Little Matlock Wheel with its dripping water and ferns, a fragment of a water level marker stone dated 1825, goits, dams, weirs, winding gear, massive blocks of masonry, scattered higgledy piggledy, in unkempt and boggy woods and even a wheel buried up at the Old Wheel!

Some of them are shown here.

Winding wheel

Weir Water Level Stone

Little Matlock Rolling Mill Wheel

Compensation Reservoir at Dam Flask embankment

Well its got to be Freddie hasn't it? But how unnerving. Whose clocking who here? Up periscopes. Brazen little bugger ain't he (or she)? Unlike the ones on the inside of Rupert Annuals.

Freddie the Frog and Lily in the Loxley Valley

The remains of Claremont House reflected in these two views are both sad and spooky. It used to be a private dwelling and then became the social club for the nearby refractories. I believe a local GP had it for a time with a view to turning it into a nursing home but it is heading for demolition and is beyond the point of no return.

Like the rest of the Hepworths site, it is impossible to secure. The view from the inside taken by your intrepid photographer is really eerie and reminds me of a scene from that scary film of the early nineteen sixties, ' The Haunting'. Brrrh.......

River Loxley

Hepworths and its dereliction is a rather sad and sorry place as well as the most controversial site in the Loxley Valley. It's no wonder that we decided not to dwell on the place too long because the nature of this book is to extol the virtues of the Loxley Valley and not to dwell on its recent industrial past, which some of us, as younger folk, thought was a scar on the place.

Now it's almost like a ghost town or abandoned mining settlement in the American West with its palleted exports to exotic destinations only a memory. It is incredible how it has become overgrown and the gloom that clings to your shoulders as you pass through it is something you would feel in your travail through Bunyan's 'Slough of Despond' and is only lightened when you enter the vicinity of the fishing pond with its lilies and life.

As the Prince of Wales said about the pre war situation of the Welsh miners, "something must be done" but what eh?

Ventnor - May 24th 1898

Cow drinking from the Old Wheel Pond

Canadian Goose on the pond

It's years since I'd seen this remarkable gravestone, in a field on the Old Wheel Farm, adjacent to the river. I'd ventured across once to view it and noted the remarkable defensive position adopted by the locals (ie cows) who had intimidated me into beating a hasty retreat (I decided I'd never watch another Ambrosia Creamed Rice advert again). Consequently when I went back with Mark I hadn't a clue where it was. Vasco Da Clayton, getting nettled, sucked into the mud and cow muck and nervous, like your esteemed photographer, about the increased interest by our bovine neighbours in our blundering about their manor. Both of us had David Blunkett's mishap in our minds. (David Blunkett had a run in with a cow whilst out walking).

"Do you mind Cowes" I said to my companion? 'I prefer Henley' he said. You can always tell a Pymm's drinker. Frequent exhortation to the herd to go away met with no response.

So bedraggled, sweaty and frustrated we staggered back to the farmhouse, much to the amusement of the farmer, who promptly sent his ten year old son to show us where the dammed thing was. Mark was less than impressed by my powers of total recall and navigational skill of a lemming whilst I was impressed by the respect the cows showed the farmer's lad.

And Ventnor? Well was he a horse or one of the Isle Of Wight Cowes? Actually a beloved gundog who went to sleep in 1898 and sleeps there still.

Cows, fascinating eyelashes and big speculative eyes. Best thing I can say about them is their cream and full fat milk tastes delicious on strawberries or ice cold on cornflakes. There is a pedigree Friesian herd commemorated in stained glass above the front door of a farmhouse by the Nag's Head.

Cows can be mistaken to be big placid beasties but understandably protective of their calves especially when a dog is about. They have been known to unnerve and worse, local MP's and timorous local scribes and photographers. Not to be regarded merely as a 'Silly Moo'. The iconic image of the British countryside and guaranteed to boost sales of tinned rice pudding and butter.

Cows crossing Rowell Lane

Lambs suckling

Cyril the Squirrel

Pen Trough at Rowell Lane

Elizabeth II Postbox on Loxley Road near the top of Rowell Lane

Telephone box at Stacey Bank

Spreading the pollen

Rowell Bridge

The bridge itself was literally swept away during the course of the 1864 Flood and its hard to believe that this quiet little country road was the scene of the case of the industrious grinder, as Sir Arthur Conan Doyle might have put it. William Bradbury, working through the night, by himself, to earn a few bob, was washed away before he knew what hit him.

Did he hear the 'clap of thunder', that Mrs. Waters(!), wife of the proprietor of the nearby Rowell Bridge Inn and flour mill, described in Harrison as announcing the arrival of the flood wave? She and her family got out via the hayloft and roof to stagger up the pitch black hillside in the early hours. How dramatic eh?

The pub is still there but is a private residence now.

Here we have photographs of Smelters Bank, showing downstream and upstream views. One of the things about the Loxley is that it is rather mysterious in parts. Many years ago, Helen Jackson, then Labour MP for Hillsborough, said to myself and Pete Quincey that she would like a foot path from Hillsborough Corner to Malin Bridge to access the Loxley Valley. Dutifully, me and Pete did a little reconnaissance and found it impossible. The banks are too steep or small or in private hands and you cannot access the riverside (the nearest they have done is behind the Park and Ride at Malin Bridge). This is true of it along its length and adds to its character and allure.

River Loxley flowing under the Smelters Bank Packhorse Bridge

So it is with Smelters Bank, just below Rowell Bridge and close by the former 19th century Rowell Bridge public house, colloquially referred to as the 'Muck Oyle'. How many people nowadays traverse the nearby packhorse bridge that leads up to Stannington?

Compared with the Rivelin, the Loxley is a much less used thoroughfare as its industry has largely died away.

Now there are records of a smelting mill and the area is referred to as Smelting Bank on the early maps but there was also a J. Smelter who bought a mill here in the early nineteenth century! The sunlight and water ripple on ancient stonework while the bridge has a datestone indicating it was rebuilt after the flood.

There is a dramatic photograph showing the pub on the front cover of Geoffrey Amey's 1974 book 'The Collapse of The Dale Dyke Dam 1864'.

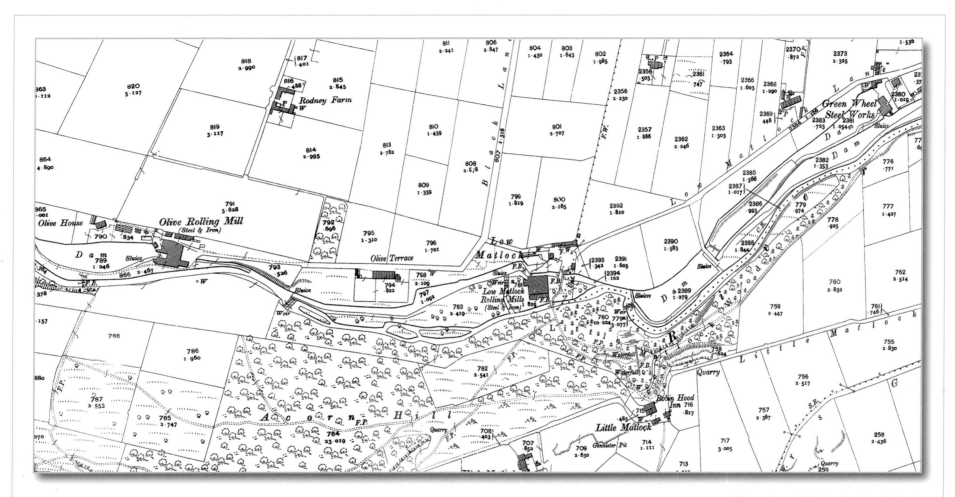

OS map from 1905 showing Low Matlock

Loxley Old Chapel

Built in 1787 and a rather brooding Brontesque structure with a number of Flood victims interred in the graveyard. The stained glass window is like all stained glass, best appreciated and seen in all its glory from the inside with the natural light streaming through. Do we no longer appreciate the beauty of stained glass because many of us never see the inside of churches or chapels?

Olive Mill Tail Goit

River Loxley at Olive Mill

Olive Mill

Cottages at Olive Terrace

The mill belongs to the council or did at one time and apparently they couldn't afford to put a roof on it. Not that it matters these days because it's quite a picturesque ruin, as long as the fabric can be maintained. Some buildings are better left that way.

As you walk up the path, opened by David Blunkett, MP, designed for the visually impaired, there's a strong scent of mint and what looks like a cutler's quenching trough buried in the ground.

Wisewood Cemetery in Winter

George V Postbox on Loxley Road
near Admiral Rodney

These photographs of Loxley show Wisewood Cemetery and the comparatively late development of Loxley as a village compared with Wamsley. I always thought it significant that there was never a Christmas tree put up at Wamsley as opposed to the one on Loxley Village Green.

What a magnificent wooded backdrop though – takes your breath away – which is how you end up in the cemetery of course.

Chapman's House site

The Robin Hood and Little John, to give it it's proper title, as George, former landlord and Wednesdayite, now retired to Bridlington, once advised me.

A piranha hung above the bar but didn't work behind it. At one time it was full of stuffed animal heads and the other paraphernalia of a country pub where dog lovers are welcome, outside memorials to customers and grindstones, Cakin Night and a drop that requires some finesse. There's another drop here to the little industrial hamlet below and a latin inscription that, together with massive stone constructions like this one, are the hallmark of the Reverend Thomas Halliday, who built it in 1804.

It was called the Rock Inn sometime in the nineteenth century and workmen trooped down the steep metalled pathway, at its rear, to the river, to the mills and forges, below, as they did across the Loxley Valley. Our reverend gentleman and his wife, Martha or Maria Patrick, who came with a handsome dowry, fancying himself a business man, built across the valley, Loxley House, and a similar edifice to the pub, (see insert left), on the flat area below what he called Cliff Rocher, known as Chapman's House. This row of cottages was damaged in the Flood with loss of life, perhaps due to its construction, the bulk of it survived. Unlike Daniel Chapman, its owner and his household.

Reverend Halliday's scheme to turn Cliff Rocher into a pleasant watering hole for the gentry floundered and he had to re-enter the Ministry to vanish into obscurity, with no issue to leave behind, a rather tragic story echoed in the translation of the inscription overlooking the valley. I am grateful again to another reverend gentleman, Dr Kirk-Smith, 'While my spirit remains, I will not leave you, O sweetest names in the world, you, O mountains, waterfalls, meadows, woods, rocks and caves'

This has to be the epitaph for all lovers of the River Loxley and its Valley.

Latin inscription at the Robin Hood Inn, Little Matlock

Nec vos. dulcissima mundi

Nomina. vos Montes. Cataractæ. Pascua. Sylvæ

Rupes atque Cavernæ. anima remanente relinquam

Thomas Halliday. 1804.

Loxley Steel Works

Loxley Steel Works gatepost

OS map from 1905 showing Wisewood and Malin Bridge

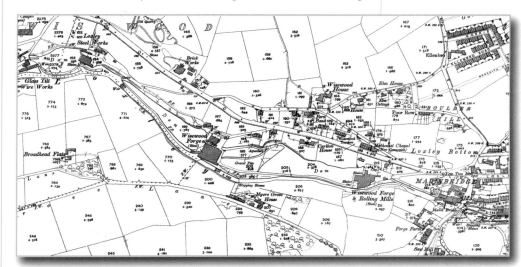

This barely decipherable stone signpost was one I remember from my boyhood days, as myself and Dave Wiggett ventured down this mysterious foliage roofed path, down to the weir where we waded across and I almost lost one shoe until Dave retrieved it. At the corner, I found a tree fern fossil which I proudly took to Weston Park to be identified (and a woodsaw). Sadly, like many things from my childhood I didn't look after it and it ended up broken in two after propping up the garden hut door at no. 24.

Further down there were concrete platforms, now overgrown, that I have thought may have been for ack-ack guns, waiting for the Luftwaffe as it returned from Manchester.

Anyhow, the steel works was built in 1868 after the Broadhead Wheel was demolished in the Flood. The name survives across the Valley as you approach the Robin Hood via the narrow lane that passes by the sorry site in more ways than one of the once renowned Pinegrove Country Club and was closed before 1931, possibly 1928, when it was moved to Attercliffe by Sir Stuart Goodwin, as he was to become.

The river flowing past Loxley Steel Works

River Loxley at the Steel Works

These images of the lower Loxley reflect the eddies and flows, brackens and rocks and unkempt trees that give it an air of the wild wood – Unutilised by man or woman and rarely trodden by him or her dog. Time stands still here and all you hear is the rush of water. You could meet the Man in Green so keep your quarterstaff handy.

Who knows you could both end up quaffing ale in the Robin Hood after a steep climb to dry off your Lincoln Green after disputing the right of way across the narrow footbridge by Olive Dam?

Rivulet at Loxley Steel Works

Wisewood Forge gatehouse

Ducks in Wisewood Forge Dam

It is sad to see this steel shuttered and vandalised, sole surviving outbuilding of Wisewood Forge. This was a quirky little dwelling once, now fallen prey to kids with too much down time on their hands and indifferent parents. I used to walk through Wisewood Forge and marvel at the bars and rolls of steel laid on the open ground with yellow and white chalk marks on. You could peer briefly into cavernous sheds and catch a glimpse of real Sheffield where people made things and grafted for a living instead of gazing into a VDU and polishing the seat of their Loxley Bottoms on a chair that meets the requirements of the Display Screen Equipment Regulations 1992.

Adjacent to this forlorn building, for whom the writing, like the graffiti, is on the wall, was the most ramshackle cottage remaining in S6.

Damaged by the flood, apparently, complete with crozzle topped boundary walls, Anderson Shelter and bracken, now replaced by a smart stone built residence which has kept much of the original stone. The Wisewood Forge Offices went a long time ago and in their place, Loxley Park, a comfortable residential home.

The original water power features are fenced off, waiting not for Godot, but planning permission.

Wisewood Forge
March 1864

Of all the pubs in the Loxley Valley, the one I should be able to wax lyrical about is the Rodney. Yet surprisingly enough I can't. That, I suspect, is because it's back in the days of the legendary Keith Ripley when I used to go in there and that's one heck of a long time ago. Keith of course goes back a long way in S6, former steward of the Dial House, then mine host of the Rodney and then the Shoulder of Mutton. His wife Joyce reminded our owd feller of Jayne Torville of ice skating fame. Keith's father was also a steward of a WMC or two in his time and, being possessed of a vigorous head of hair, was nicknamed 'Rug 'eard'.

This magnificent Copper Beech Tree was planted in 1935 to celebrate the Silver Jubilee of King George V.

King George's last words on his deathbed were supposedly either 'How is the Empire?' or 'Bugger Bognor'! I prefer the latter version.

This rather singular stone on Loxley Village Green is called the mounting stone, which you used presumably for getting on your horse. It was moved from across the road apparently.

There was a hitching post some years ago up near the old ganister mines where you presumably tied your horse to (or scratched your back) whether it's true or not, who knows.

In those days it had a nautical flavour with prints of sailing ships and battle ships and imitation brassware including a warming pan on which I used to do a pretty appalling impression of George Formby and Lonnie Donnigan. Those were the days when Stones's were Stooones!

Nowadays the Rodney is an eating out venue compared to when I entered its portals as a regular, I recently

enjoyed a pint or two of real ale outside, in what cannot be remotely called a beer garden but more a viewing area across the valley. In doing so you invariably find yourself commiserating with the smoking fraternity but rather relieved that they aren't inside, which seems a bit hypocritical.

The Old Rodney, nearer to the road, had a blacksmith's forge in its vicinity which survived until my time as a regular. Admiral Rodney was a renowned seadog of the eighteenth century who exchanged broadsides with both the French and Spanish Navies.

Mounting Stone

Loxley House, built in 1795 - the former Headquarters of the Sheffield Sea Cadets

A derelict Pinegrove

Pinegrove Country Club

The Wisewood Inn, formerly several cottages knocked together and a cosy, intimate, place with a panoramic view over the valley. Hard to define the boundaries of the original Wisewood as it seems to have taken over great swathes of Sheffield 6.

I've passed through the Pinegrove's portals and the characters I've seen include: Brendan Ingle, Mad Frankie Fraser, Martin Hodge, Prince Nazeem, Gerry, Pat Proctor – some of whom have now gone to that great country club in the sky. The Pinegrove is very much a child of its times and like the Dial House Club, someone ought to write its story.

The best quote on Pinegrove: "A country club for the working man" as recounted by the man best fitted to write the story – Geoff Beattie.

Yew Tree Inn

Built about 1850 and badly damaged in 1864, the Corn Mill was known locally as German Wilson's. The earliest reference to a wheel on the site is 1739. *The wheel is pictured below.*

A variety of occupiers and uses over the years thus reflecting the changing times and fortunes of my beloved Loxley Bottoms – Comet, Charlie Wades Restaurant, Designer Gear Shop etc.

The wheel was renovated in the 1970's, and it seems to have taken an eternity to restore it fully. It is a rarity being undershot ie water goes under the wheel.

Your's truly has been tasked with the job of setting up a local volunteers group to turn the wheel and keep it in good nick.

Corn Mill Wheel

The Yew Tree Inn is quite a striking edifice at the bottom of Dykes Lane, or as it was formerly known, Boulder Hill. I have spent considerable time on its steps contemplating Loxley Bottoms and in the early evening, the lights of the Supper Spot.

Now the Yew Tree goes back, at least to 1802, when the Fairbanks surveyed the area. The original building was used as a venue for a coroner's inquest after the flood. When I first knew it, Gary and Jane used to run it and there were some tiles or prints of local scenes of the aftermath of the disaster. Probably ended up in a skip.

As for its name, well yew trees were planted in churchyards to keep evil spirits away, and also so you had a ready supply of wood for the longbow.

Used of course by one Robin of Loxley.

It is some time since I have seen this memorial to the Malin Bridge victims of the Great Flood. It is on white marble with black lettering and typically Victorian, solemn, reverential and I suppose, to the modern eye, rather 'heavy' in substance as well as style. Yet it tells a very human story, whole families wiped out in an inkling. Some names and stories forgotten, some remembered, handed down, generation by generation, to this day. Like the Victorian wooden battledore bat, found in the mud at either Hillsborough Corner or Malin Bridge and kept in the family until handed over to me, a mere stranger. The kids were never allowed to play with it, unlike its original owner, whose name and fate is unknown. It is now in Kelham Island Museum where it thankfully survived a later flood and you can see it illustrated by Eric Leslie in Peter Machan's book on the Flood.

The tablet itself was 'erected by public subscription' and is by one,' I. Ollerenshaw', which is a name I have seen on gravestones in the valley.

Maybe we need a more modern memorial. This one was once in St Mark's in Dykes Lane and moved to St. Polycarps, where it is now in situ, at an unknown date and for an unknown reason. Was it first erected in the former Methodist New Connection Chapel of 1832, now workshops for both motor vehicles and wrought ironwork?

Somebody clear that one up for me. Any idea what its date is?

Either way Malin Bridge witnessed the greatest loss of life in one spot because most folk were asleep and unaware of the concern up at the windswept embankment plus the valley sides were steep and forced the water down with great destructive force.

Malin Bridge and Corn Mill circa 1900

In August 2009, a £250,000 scheme of flood management improvements began at Malin Bridge. Over the following couple of months, trees were felled and debris removed to reveal views not seen for more than sixty years. The original weir below Malin Bridge was restored to its former glory as well as the dam and sluice on the other side of Rivelin Valley Road Bridge.

The River Loxley has never flowed better!

Malin Bridge and Corn Mill during clean up

Edward VII Postbox at Oakwood Road

Malin Bridge Inn

Flood Trail Plaque

The Shakey

If anywhere in the Loxley Valley is a repository of scenes of the aftermath of the Great Sheffield Flood, it is here in the best rooms of this traditional and much loved beerhouse. Notice also the legend affixed, by the front door, of the drowned George Bisby and his household in the 'Cleakum' Inn. Well that's one version but why 'Cleakum'? Well 'Cleakum' is an old Yorkshire phrase meaning to 'snatch at' and you can imagine the thirsty colliers, labourers and workmen grabbing their foaming tankards to wash away the dust and slake their thirst. Beware the beer thief as they say! And what of the story that mine hostess with the mostess, Jane Gordon-Revett, told me about the friendly ghost (Casper by any chance?) who used to wake her children up? But there's always spirits in pubs, you know.

And that's not all the mystery. Look at the images of Malin Bridge – is the imposing roof that of the Malin? Look at the front elevation of the pub. Where have you seen that before outside the pages of this book? Isn't it very similar to that of the Shakey? Now we know that establishment survived the flood. So did the Malin? Oh and I should have mentioned another harmless apparition of these parts ... the lady in crinoline garb further down the road near ... but my lips are sealed on that one ... oops!

Malin Bridge after the clean up ▶

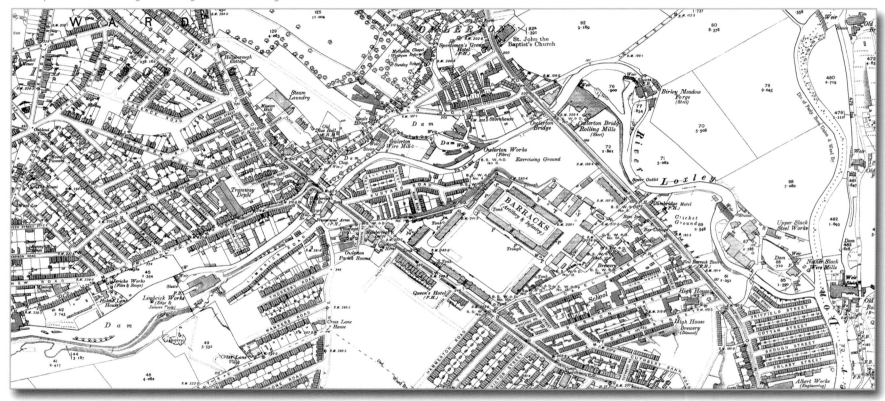

Standing on the pavement on Walkley Lane and looking across to Hillsborough Corner, one's attention is drawn inevitably to the river and weir which served three wheels and which remains in good condition. Back when they were preparing the area for the advent of Supertram, a JCB was running amok and damaging the weir. Thankfully we spotted what was happening and got it stopped. On the left hand side the weir is very deep and it is only when water levels are abnormally low that you can see it. Of course everyone looks over the bridge and it's a bit like the Generation Game Conveyor Belt. 'Cuddly Toy, Percolator, Settee, Tyre, Shopping Trolley etc'.

Some years back, myself and John Hatfield of Mousehole Forge rescued the 1826 datestone from the buildings of Upper Owlerton Wheel (where the shopping precinct is now on the right hand side of Bradfield Road and just before Regent Court Flats). Sadly we didn't manage to save the window arches (which vanished overnight) or take a photograph of the workshops themselves or save the enamelled shop signs that were in them! Well at least the datestone is saved for posterity in the Mousehole.

Old Park Silver Rolling Mill

As Prospero says 'Our revels now are ended'. Our Odyssey down the Loxley is over and on a rather sad note, but only briefly.

There I was the other night in the Freemasons at Hillsborough when I noticed they have extended the height of the railings by the riverside to stop people throwing themselves over. Why? The Credit Crunch? Wednesday's results? The most intimate view of the Loxley down its length is spoiled. The adjacent bridge painted black over the faded floral design that was the work of Hillsborough Community Development Trust and by the pub's riverside wall, a reminder of the varied species of fish that the Loxley sustains. Ah well, there's always hope...

Anyhow, its not been a straightforward journey, as Odysseus found out: bits here and there, and memories from younger days. It's been fascinating, sweaty, thirsty and tiring work, has Ron and Mark's 'Big Adventure'.

And here it is, where the River Loxley meets the River Don and how appropriate here, not far from World's End or Wardsend, the photo being taken from the Old Park Silver Rolling Mill on Club Mill Road.

On the left, the Loxley is a different hue to the Don or Dun as they used to call it. Off flows the Don to pass under the buried remains of Sheffield Castle and to link up with the Sheaf at Blonk Street.
But that is another story as they say...

George VI Postbox
at Bradfield Road

Edward VIII Postbox
at Law Bros petrol
station

River Loxley confluence with River Don

Ron Clayton (the wordsmith)

Is the original Professional Sheffielder. He has been many things in his life (cheerful isn't one of them). For the last thirty five years, in particular, a square peg in a round hole.

Allergic to fish, yet the son of a fishmonger, he has described his forty five years and more of watching Sheffield Wednesday as 'Victory Into Defeat' and has been described as a 'reactionary', 'a dinosaur' and 'politically incorrect' but prefers the usual description 'good company'. Ron fancies Lulu, Lesley Garrett, Pam Grier and Janet Leigh, in her heyday, but it is unlikely that these feelings are reciprocated, especially in the case of Janet Leigh.

He has been known to prowl the Loxley Valley dressed as Friar Tuck.

Says it all really.

Mark Rodgers (the lensman)

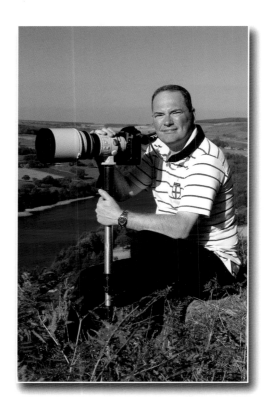

Mark has been a professional photographer for more than 20 years. He started his own businesss in the late 1980s after completing a diploma in photography at Blackpool and Fylde College.

A Sheffield Six resident all his life, although a Unitedite, he hopes that this book will inspire all who turn its pages to explore and discover more about this magnificent tract of land many people call their home.